KLIMT

THE GREAT ARTISTS COLLECTION

MASON CREST

Contents

2

*Great Works order is alphabetical where possible.

KLIMT

Mason Crest
450 Parkway Drive, Suite D
Broomall, PA 19008
www.masoncrest.com

©2016 by Mason Crest, an imprint of National Highlights, Inc.

Printed and bound in the United States of America.

10 9 8 7 6 5 4 3 2 1

Cataloging-in-Publication Data on file with the Library of Congress.

Series ISBN: 978-1-4222-3256-9
Hardback ISBN: 978-1-4222-3260-6
ebook ISBN: 978-1-4222-8537-4

Written by: Sara Haynes

Images courtesy of PA Photos and Scala Archives

"All art is erotic."
Gustav Klimt

Introduction

(Mary Evans/Epic/PVDE)

■ **ABOVE: Gustav Klimt, c. 1905.**

In the later part of the 19th century and the first two decades of the 20th century, Gustav Klimt (1862-1918) was a forerunner of the Art Nouveau movement in Vienna, Austria. Also known in Germany as "youth style," this new movement brought forth one of the most decorative, leading European artists, and greatest exponent of erotic art that the world had ever seen.

Klimt began his career as a highly renowned academic painter, but he was propelled toward the greater modern trends in art, which saw a development of the erotic,

fantastical, and eclectic. This led Klimt to co-found the Vienna Secession – a movement dedicated to those artists who resigned from the establishment (The Association of Austrian Artists) – where he became its first president. At the start of his career, the Austrian artist was commissioned to paint a number of public buildings, producing friezes and murals. However, the development of his own style would lead him to scandal and accusations that his works were distasteful and pornographic in their portrayal of his themes and motifs. Klimt steadily moved away from the historical and mythical subjects (and an established style of the 19th century), which dominated many of his early works, in search of a realism that would see him produce some of the most precise, almost photographic, portraits and great works, while pursuing his interest in the decorative and ornate. He was a great believer in fine and decorative art – despite the reticence of some of his contemporaries – and strove to bring about a union of the visual arts, created through ornamental elements. Klimt worked closely with the design studio, Wiener Werkstatte, (founded in 1903) in order to ensure an improvement in the quality of everyday objects and the form of applied arts. Some Impressionist influences are evident in Klimt's work, but generally he developed a style of his own, matched by few, which while perhaps not making as much of an impact on modern and contemporary art as the likes of Paul Cézanne and Vincent Van Gogh, and later, Salvador Dali, has played a significant role nevertheless. Klimt was greatly influenced by Greek, Egyptian, and Byzantine art (evidence of which is found in works of his Golden Period or Phase), and he borrowed a number of motifs from these mediums. Klimt is often described as a Symbolist painter – and many of his works do contain a depth of Symbolism – however, he was also allusive to the movement. Another renowned feature of Klimt's works is his treatment of the erotic; he had a considerable healthy interest in sex (it is reported he fathered at least 14 children), but he was careful to depict women delicately, honorably, and with respect.

The Vienna Secession was founded April 3, 1897. The founding members included Klimt, Koloman Moser, Josef Hoffman, Joseph Maria Olbrich, and Max Kurzweil. Later, Otto Wagner joined the group. The idea behind the Secession was to move away from the conservative and traditional Vienna Kunstlerhaus and its historicism, and the first exhibition was held in the year following its inauguration. French Impressionists were favored by the Secession and did a great deal to bring the movement to Austria. While the exhibitions proved popular, it was the fourteenth show that would bring the most success. With Klimt's *The Beethoven Frieze,* mounted on three walls, and a statue of the Classical and Romantic German composer by Max Klinger in the center of the room, it was a roaring success. The artists involved with the Vienna Secession were not tied by one particular style (as most other new movements tended to be), and all styles and influences were acceptable to the group. At the heart of the Secession was its building in Vienna, where above the door, the words "Der Zeit ihre Kunst. Der Kunst ihre Freiheit." ("To every age its art. To art its freedom.") were displayed.

(Public Domain)

■ ABOVE: The Vienna Secession Hall in Vienna.

■ **ABOVE:** A sales outlet for the Wiener Werkstatte who Klimt worked closely with.

■ **RIGHT:** Joseph Maria Olbrich (on the left), an unknown person, Koloman Moser, and Gustav Klimt (on the right) in the garden of Fritz Waerndorfer in Vienna, c. 1898.

■ **BELOW:** The January edition of the *Ver Sacrum* magazine in 1898.

Built in 1898, and designed by Joseph Maria Olbrich, the Secession was found in Karlsplatz, and was quickly known as simply "The Secession." Historical influences were out; the first writings of Freud and the creativity of the individual artists, architects, and sculptures were in. The group had its own magazine, *Ver Sacrum*, which furthered the movement's exploration of art outside the strict confines of academic tradition. Other artists involved included Arnold

(Mary Evans Picture Library/Imagno)

Bocklin, Eugene Grasset, and Charles Rennie Mackintosh. However, following differences of opinion over artistic concepts, Klimt and a number of other artists left the Secession on June 14, 1905.

Symbolism began as a literary concept, but was soon to be found in the works of painters, particularly those who rejected the conventions of Naturalism. These painters believed that art should reflect an emotion or idea, rather than the natural world in an objective sense. It was believed that the symbolic value or meaning of a work of art stemmed from the emotional experiences of the audience, through color, line, and composition. This led to imaginary dream worlds populated with Biblical characters and figures from Greek mythology. There was a focus on love, sexual awakening, desire, fear, anguish, and death, and women became a favored symbol – as

(Mary Evans Picture Library/Imagno)

a way of expressing universal emotions – often appearing as virginal, mythical, or femme fatales. From the final two decades of the 19th century, through to the first decade of the 20th century, this was what embodied the art of the Symbolists. Klimt was no different. Symbolists tended to represent a diverse group of artists, who worked independently with varying goals – though there was a move to escape from reality, and abstract forms became popular with broad brushstrokes of color, which remained flat. Symbolism began in France, but it spread across Europe and North America from the early 1880s. Edvard Munch was closely associated with Symbolist circles,

while Klimt took elements of Symbolism and applied them by revealing his fascination with the productive and destructive forces of female sexuality. Klimt successfully brought together the elements of Symbolism with the decorative nature of Art Nouveau. Klimt is particularly noted for his paintings, murals, sketches, and other art and was prolific in Vienna at a time of great change. Many forms of culture gravitated toward the city by the turn of the century. Pioneering developments in literature, architecture, and music, alongside the arts, were taking place and, in 1910, Vienna was the fifth-largest city in the world. It was the undisputed cultural capital of Central

(Public Domain)

■ **ABOVE:** *Self-portrait of Hans Makart*, a 19th-century Austrian academic history painter, designer, and decorator.

■ **LEFT:** The Vienna Secession exhibition's main hall. A collective exhibition by Gustav Klimt, with interior design by Kolo Moser. Vienna, 1903.

11

Europe and Klimt's works served to reflect the discoveries across all genres and mediums surrounding him at this time. Society was undergoing dramatic changes and Klimt's fascination with, and depictions of, women reveal the emergence of a more liberal, confident, middle class. His total works reflect the evolution of artistic movements and he was greatly influenced by the likes of Hans Makart (the defining Viennese painter of the late 19th century). Klimt's most successful and financially profitable time came during his Golden Period, or Gold Phase, in the early 1900s with works such as *The Kiss*, possibly his most famous painting.

Klimt

A Biography

(Mary Evans Picture Library/Imagno)

■ **ABOVE:** Gustav Klimt holding one of his cats in front of his studio at Josefstaedter Strasse 21 in the 8th district, Vienna.

Born in Baumgarten, near Vienna in Austria-Hungary on July 14, 1862, Gustav Klimt was the second of seven children. His siblings consisted of two younger brothers and four sisters. His father, Ernst Klimt Sr., was a gold engraver originally from Bohemia, while his mother, Anna, had wanted to be a performer. Her musical ambitions remained unrealized. All three Klimt brothers had artistic talents – Gustav, Ernst Jr., and Georg would later work together. It was a particularly tough existence for the family. Work in the Habsburg Empire – particularly for immigrants – was scarce. The family moved often – always in search of cheaper housing. This was combined with personal family tragedy. Anna, Klimt's five-year-old younger sister, died in 1874 following a long illness. This was closely followed by the mental breakdown of another sister, Klara. On an academic level, Gustav Klimt was doing well and was singled out by his teachers as an exceptional draftsman. He was encouraged to take the entrance exam for the Viennese Schools of Arts and Crafts, which he passed with distinction.

Klimt attended Kunstgewerbeschule (the Vienna School of Arts), where he studied architectural painting, up to 1883. It was here, while living in abject poverty and accepting a formal conservative training, that the artist developed his passion for the likes of Hans Makart. His traditional study, at the now Austrian Museum of Applied Art/Contemporary Art (MAK), helped to propel Klimt as one of Europe's leading academic painters and he was comfortable with this at the time. His brother Ernst also joined the school and, like their father, became an engraver. He had left school early – along with his brother – in order to provide for the family following the economic crash of 1873. This financial support was to continue for Klimt's family throughout his life.

(Public Domain)

■ ABOVE: **The staircase of the Burgtheater, Vienna.**

■ **ABOVE:** A parade in Vienna in 1879 for the 25th wedding anniversary of Austrian sovereigns Emperor Franz Joseph I and Empress Elisabeth of Bavaria organized by Hans Makart.

Klimt's conservative training took place in the Ringstrasse Era – a time when Vienna was undergoing dramatic changes, which saw the Bourgeois class patronizing the arts far more than ever before. There were also huge technological developments underway, with the introduction of the railway and electric streetlights, while the River Danube was rerouted in order to avoid the persistent threat of flooding. Industry, research, and science were entering a Golden Age, but sadly, the arts were yet to become part of this great revolution.

In 1879, under the direction of Hans Makart, Gustav and Ernst – together with Franz Matsch – were commissioned to organize a procession for the silver wedding of Emperor Franz Joseph I and his wife, Empress Elisabeth, while four years later, the three young men founded the Kunstler-Compagnie. The collective wall paintings that followed were based on sketches by Makart and proved the first time that Klimt used gold in his sketches. Together with Ernst and Matsch, Klimt began work on the frescoes for the staircases of the Burgtheater in 1886. Two years later, the work was completed and Klimt and his two companions began to finalize Hans Makart's unfinished decoration of the Kunsthistorisches Museum. His painting here, *Innenansicht des alten K.K. Hofburgtheaters,* won him the Kaiser Prize. The recognition that Klimt was by now gaining would see him commissioned – along with Matsch – to paint works for the University of Vienna (including *Medicine, Philosophy,* and *Jurisprudence* – see Great Works). However, these works – due to the treatment of the subjects and themes – were viewed as obscene, pornographic, and caused a huge scandal amongst Vienna's elite, as well as the establishment. The government commissions were rejected.

By this time, his father and brother, Ernst, had died (both in 1892) and he had been obligated to take on the financial responsibilities for both families. In 1897, Klimt left the Kunstlerhaus in order to co-found the Vienna Secession. However, his works at the first and second exhibitions caused further controversy for Klimt, but he redeemed himself and found himself in much demand when he presented his large square portrait of Viennese socialite Sonja Knips. It was to be the start of a number of commissions from high-profile, wealthy patrons and would establish Klimt as a prolific exponent of portraitures. In 1900, at the seventh Secession exhibition, Klimt showed his landscapes for the first time. These were to prove extremely popular, with their careful and considered brushstrokes, abundance of flowers, and the artist's obvious love and understanding of nature. While *Philosophy* received a horrified reception, this was also the

year in which the World Exhibition in Paris voted it as the best and Klimt was presented with the Gold Medal.

Whether Klimt met his lifelong companion in the late 1890s or early 1900s is unclear – there are differing reports, however, he first painted a portrait of Emilie Flöge in 1902. The fashion designer – despite his relationships with other women and the birth of at least 14 children fathered by the artist – was to remain close to him for the remainder of his life. Neither Flöge, nor her mother, were particularly taken with the portrait – a beautiful and serene portraiture (see Great Works). Klimt and Flöge collaborated together on designs for clothes for Flöge's boutique, situated on Mariahilfer Strasse, Vienna. By the following year the artist had become involved in the newly created Wiener Werkstatte – dedicated to the form of fine arts – which, in time, would go on to be greatly influenced by him.

In 1904, Klimt designed the frieze for the dining room of Palais Stoclet (today these designs are housed on display in the MAK). In 1906, The Association of Austrian Artists was founded. (Six years later, in 1912, Klimt became its president.) The following year, in 1907, his portrait of Fritza Riedler formed part of his Golden Period, as did his painting of Adele Bloch-Bauer (now one of the most expensive works in the world). This was also the year that *The Kiss* was created – displayed for the first time in 1908 – it is undoubtedly one of Klimt's most well-known and popular paintings. *Death and Life* (c. 1910) won first prize at the International Exhibition of Art in Rome. It is around this time that the artist moved to his final studio in Vienna (now a memorial to Klimt).

Very little is really known of Klimt's personal life – he was essentially a private man. While he loved lavish fashions, he was generally found in a smock, minus any undergarments, working from morning until night. It is virtually impossible to tell from his few letters and postcards and the photographs of him that survived whether his companion, Emilie Flöge, was his lover or just a close friend. He chose not to divulge the information, although it is known that he enjoyed a passionate relationship with Alma Schindler before she married the composer, and Klimt's musical contemporary, Gustav Mahler. Emilie's letters to Klimt were destroyed by her sister (widow of Ernst Klimt) but there is evidence to suggest from the artist's letters and cards to his lifelong companion that he loved her. Some suspect that the love was unrequited. We do know, however, that the artist was not a Marxist and was comfortable with both glamour and money – his later paintings were to become extremely expensive. Klimt was a great admirer of cats and often had many of them in his studios. It is believed that he thought their urine was

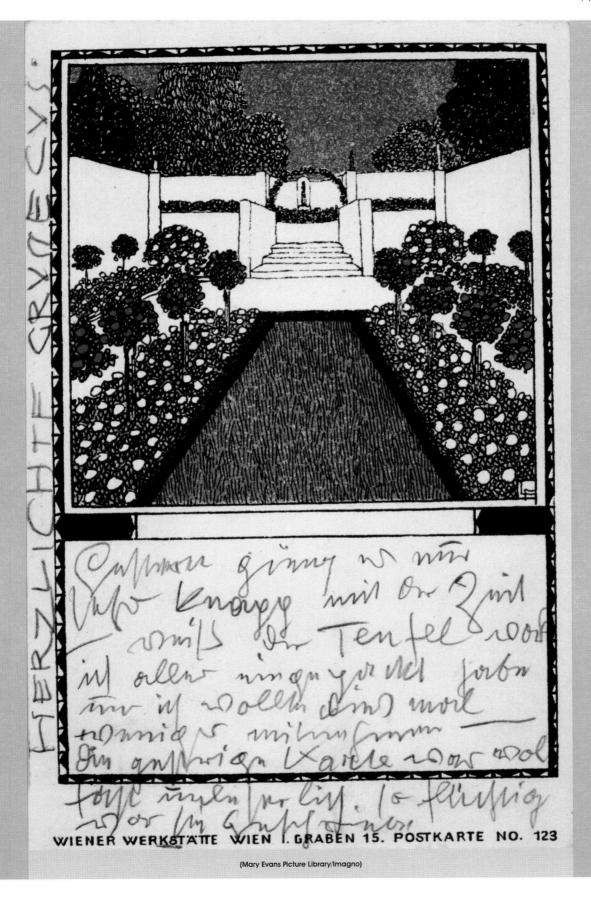

■ **ABOVE:** A postcard written by Gustav Klimt to Emilie Flöge.

■ **ABOVE:** Emilie Flöge in a dress designed by Gustav Klimt. This photograph was taken at the Attersee in 1906.

(Mary Evans Picture Library/Imagno)

■ **ABOVE: Gustav Klimt, aged 55, one year before his death. This is one of the last photographs of Klimt and was taken by Moriz Naehr, 1917.**

the best fixative around. In turn, this gave Klimt a rather animal-like odor, which was repellent to some; it does seem to have put women off this small, chunky man, who was said to have an incredible sexual appetite. He carried on many intense and tempestuous relationships with his models and patrons alike. Although at least 14 illegitimate children are known to have been fathered by Klimt, there are estimates that another two children were fathered at some point. Eventually, Klimt developed syphilis and was unable to take part physically in sexual activity. This has prompted a number of commentators to state that this is

why his later works had more overt sexual content – they provided a form of release – but perhaps it is more likely that he was just as equally fascinated by the visual as he was the physical. Whatever the private life of this great man, his works leave behind a legacy that is enduring and strong. He changed the face of art in a formal, conservative Vienna and brought to life the joy of love, beauty, and awakening.

Gustav Klimt died on February 6, 1918 following illness in the wake of the world's influenza outbreak, which killed millions.

Great Works

Paintings

Adam and Eve

(1917-1918)

• Oil on canvas, unfinished, 68.1 in x 63 in (173 cm x 160 cm)

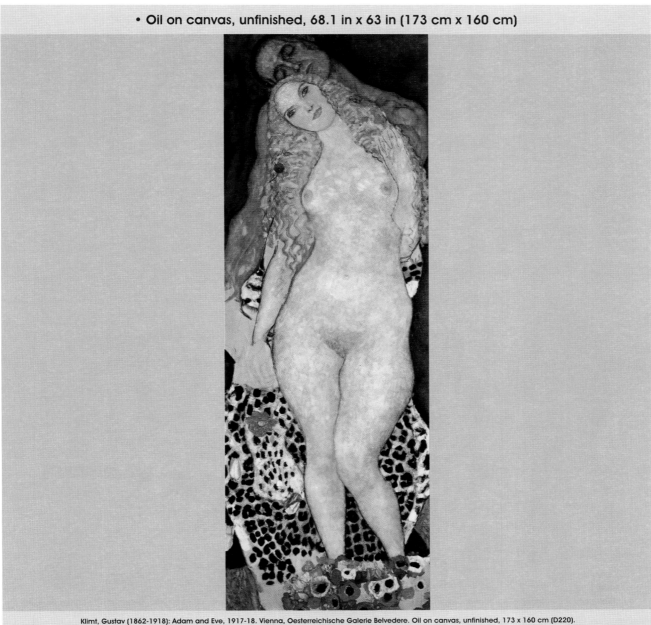

Klimt, Gustav (1862-1918): Adam and Eve, 1917-18. Vienna, Oesterreichische Galerie Belvedere. Oil on canvas, unfinished, 173 x 160 cm (D220).
© 2013. Photo Austrian Archives/Scala, Florence

This exquisite work shows Klimt's love of women, with Eve, portrayed here as goddess-like, beautiful, and serene. She exudes calmness and is an ethereal presence against the darker backdrop of Adam. He, in turn, shadows Eve and his contours follow hers in harmony. It appears here that he has no importance for the artist. It is Eve that dominates the painting and is the important figure of the piece. The darker hues and background of the painting do not detract from the pale beauty of this Biblical depiction, which gives the woman a gentler, dignified powerfulness than Eve might otherwise have been given. Klimt was renowned for his depictions of the naked female form. He preferred the female anatomy and its aesthetics compared to the male form and was considerate and delicate in his paintings of women. For Klimt to focus on a Biblical scene was unusual – he was not remotely religious – however, this unfinished painting, due to the artist's untimely death from the pandemic influenza that struck the globe following the First World War (1914-1918), is a peaceful painting of love and dominance working in harmony.

Avenue in the Park of Kammer Castle
(1912)

• Oil on canvas, 39.4 in x 39.4 in (100 cm x 100 cm)

Klimt, Gustav (1862-1918): Tree-lined road leading to the manor house at Kammer, Upper Austria (1912). Vienna, Oesterreichische Galerie Belvedere. Oil on canvas, 100 x 100 cm.
© 2013. Photo Austrian Archives/Scala, Florence

This work, *Avenue in the Park of Kammer Castle*, is one of Klimt's more traditional pieces, which it could be argued is in the Post-Impressionist style. The artist is not renowned for Post-Impressionism – it lacks the gold and bright colors more widely associated with Klimt and his Golden Period – yet this tree-lined cobbled road down toward the castle is intricate and captivating in its composition. The trees, in terms of their branches, leaves, and thick trunks, dominate the piece, which shows the yellow walls of the castle at the end of a canopied avenue. The small "window" of sky above the patches of red roof, just visible through the trees, gives some light to a piece which might possibly otherwise be overbearing.

The trees frame each side of the painting with dark trunks leading to the lush green leaves at the top of the work. The trunks are surrounded by the green hues of the grass, also leading down to the barely visible castle and its bright walls and dark gate. This later painting (completed in 1912) is composed of carefully worked (and somewhat hidden) brushstrokes. It is a masterpiece of harmony and interpretation.

Birch Forest
(1903)

• Oil on canvas, 43.3 x 43.3 in (110 x 110 cm)

Klimt, Gustav (1862-1918): Birkenwald/Buchenwald (Birch Forest / Beech Forest), 1903. Oil on canvas. Formerly Vienna, Oesterreichisches Galerie im Belvedere, auctioned at Christie's 2006 (Bloch-Bauer heirs' legal action). © 2013. Photo Austrian Archives/Scala, Florence

This carefully crafted piece shows Klimt's love of the tranquility of forests and woods. The painting pays homage to the earth, forest floor, and lean trees rather than to the vegetation at the top. Some citations with regard to this enchanting work mention that without the treetops and sky – which here are left to the imagination – the work could be considered claustrophobic in its outlook. However, the artist has cleverly combined the green, brown, gray, and red hues to create a painting that balances the nature of the lower part of the forest without the need for anything further to explain or give light or breath to the piece. It is a light, almost fall-like interpretation of the forest. The work is a shimmering depiction of peace and solitude in a beautiful surrounding. Many commentators believe that forests are dark, dank places that exclude light by the very nature of the trees that inhabit them, yet in reality, forests are magical places with light-filled canopies, where that light is allowed to filter toward the ground and the carpet of leaves that literally obliterate the forest floor for a number of months each year. Both the trunks of the trees and the red/brown leaves are painted with careful strokes in order to give movement and life. It is suggested that Grimm's fairy tales and the heritage of folklore based around forests gave Klimt the inspiration for this painting, which sold at Christie's for $40,336,000 in November 2006. It was originally owned by Adele and Ferdinand Bloch-Bauer, but following the Nazi Annex of Austria in March 1938, was seized by the Viennese Magistrate. It was returned to its rightful heirs 68 years later in 2006, just a few months before it was sold at auction.

Death and Life

(c. 1910)

• Oil on canvas, 70.1 in x 78 in (178 cm x 198 cm)

Klimt, Gustav (1862-1918): Death and Life, c. 1910. Oil on canvas, 178 x 198 cm (D183). © 2013. Photo Austrian Archives/Scala, Florence

The never-ending "circle of life," watched by an allegorical Grim Reaper, is represented in this typical work by Klimt, where symbols take center stage. Life is covered by each and every generation, from the small baby to the elderly woman; but with life comes death. The painting is not a personal representation of life and death, but a vision of the artist's view on the subject with regard to humanity. The patterned garment of "Death," with its black, blue, green, purple crossed and circular hues, is balanced by the colorful circular patterns surrounding humanity to the right of the piece. The main symbol chosen to accompany the death figure is the cross. The patterns are almost textile in their approach, like flowerbeds – Klimt was renowned for his interest in costumes – and while he does not "dress" humanity, he does surround them with materials and color. The figures chosen to represent life are mainly women. While the baby and another figure are clearly male, women dominate the picture. Whether this is because Klimt preferred the female form, or saw women as the source of life, is unclear.

The work was recognized at the International Art Exhibition in Rome in 1911 when it received first prize. Klimt had described the piece as his most important figurative work, but began reworking the painting in 1915 (even though it was framed).

Expectation
(1905-1909)

• Watercolor on paper, 76.2 in x 45.3 in (193.5 cm x 115 cm)

Expectation, preparatory cartoon for the Stoclet Frieze, 1905-1909, by Gustav Klimt (1862-1918). Vienna, Upper Belvedere. © 2013. DeAgostini Picture Library/Scala, Florence

Originally entitled *The Dancer,* this watercolor, *Expectations,* is clearly based on Egyptian influences – note the upper body and head of the woman. Her arms and hands are positioned in a way reminiscent of Egyptian art, while it is suggested that this also gives a depiction of what was a dance pose of the time. While this work is a watercolor on paper, the piece was contained within a huge mosaic that adorned three walls of the Palais Stoclet in Brussels. Built by Josef Hoffmann between 1905 and 1911, and owned by banker Adolphe Stoclet, who had met the Austrian architect during the years he lived in Vienna, the building represented the ideals of the Vienna Workshop. Klimt's mosaic was designed for the dining room and worked in total harmony with Hoffmann's vision of "the total work of art," or "Gesamthunstwerk."

Expectation was produced by creating a life-sized drawing on tracing paper and attaching it to marble plates. The pencil marks were then transferred to the stone through the collaboration of marble workers, enamellers, and gilders, all working to strict instructions from the artist.

Fable

(1883)

• Oil on canvas, 33.3 in x 46 in (84.5 cm x 117 cm)

Klimt, Gustav (1862-1918): The fairy tale, 1883. Oil on canvas. © 2013. Photo Austrian Archives/Scala, Florence

Here, even in this early work, Klimt is giving rise to the female heroine, who is surrounded by adoring animals in a wooded backdrop. The woman is the dominant figure who accepts the adoration from her audience as her right. For their part, the animals appear almost lifelike in their relaxed positions – particularly note the lion. The woman, however, while beautiful and serene, looks fairly posed – almost as if she is the unreal "fable" of the piece. The painting, aptly named *Fable*, where animals were very much part of the story, was part of the first two installments of paintings commissioned by Martin Gerlach, a publisher, intent on reviving Renaissance, Baroque, and Rococo art. The three-part collection was entitled *Allegories, Emblems and Allegory: New Series.* The final collection was produced 10 years later than the first two. Klimt, it is believed, was highly influenced by historical painter, Hans Makart.

Goldfish
(1901-1902)

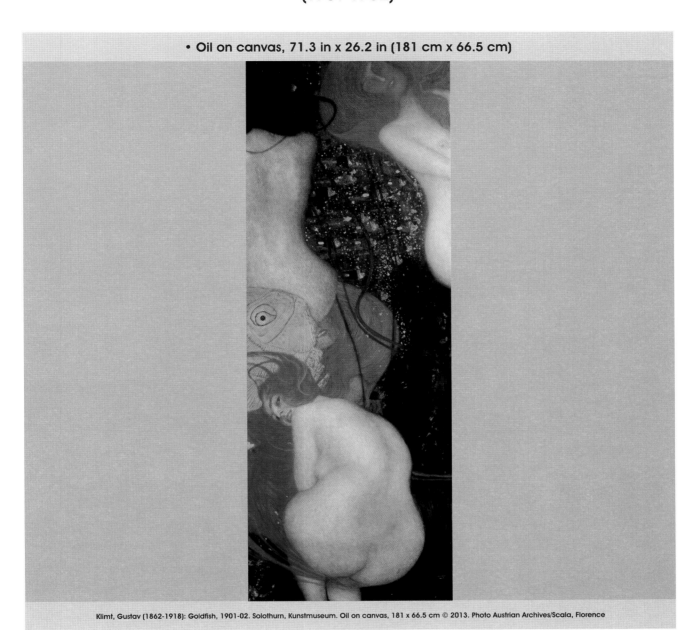

• Oil on canvas, 71.3 in x 26.2 in (181 cm x 66.5 cm)

Klimt, Gustav (1862-1918): Goldfish, 1901-02. Solothurn, Kunstmuseum. Oil on canvas, 181 x 66.5 cm © 2013. Photo Austrian Archives/Scala, Florence

With its underwater scene, naked figures, and almost joker-like goldfish, this piece was highly controversial when it was unveiled in the early 20th century. However, the naked woman to the fore of this painting, and more markedly, her naked bottom, is Klimt's comment on what he thought of his critics who had described his commissioned pieces for the ceiling at the University of Vienna as pornographic. Klimt had been commissioned by the Austrian government to create paintings for the great hall, within the university, but *Philosophy*, *Medicine*, and *Jurisprudence* were deemed completely unacceptable by the authorities, both in government and at the university, and none of the paintings were included. Presented in 1900, (he was commissioned in 1894) the works were immediately rejected and Klimt refused all subsequent government commissions. While painting *Goldfish*, Klimt was more convinced than ever of a need for the Vienna Secession. Painted during his Golden Period, the work was a defiant retaliation on the part of the artist against the establishment. Around this time, as well as using gold to symbolize sacred objects, Klimt was interested in using gold to express sexual appeal. This particular work was one of his early pieces, which combined the erotic with sensual art. It was a form expressing happiness in harmony with sexual connotations.

Hope I

(1903)

• Oil on canvas, 74.5 in x 26.4 in (189.2 cm x 67 cm)

This highly symbolic depiction of a pregnant woman widely perplexed Klimt's critics when it was completed in 1903. It wasn't the first time that the artist had used a pregnant figure (*Medicine,* the second of three paintings for the ill-fated University project had also disclosed a pregnant woman), however, the subject matter was confusing and, quite frankly, unacceptable to audiences of the time. It simply went against all propriety at the turn of the 20th century. The work has a life and death balance: the pregnant woman with the backdrop of death depicted in gaunt hooded figures and the skull. Despite the threatening nature of the backdrop of the painting, the woman remains calm and focused. The woman is unafraid and shows courage and conviction even though she is surrounded by death. She portrays serenity and beauty amidst the ugly, taking comfort from her condition. In early sketches for this work, a couple was depicted in happiness. It is thought that the darker, dramatic change in this daring painting came as a result of Klimt's feelings with regard to the death of his infant son in 1902.

Judith I

(1901)

• Oil on canvas, 33.1 in x 16.5 in (84 cm x 42 cm)

Judith I, 1901, by Gustav Klimt (1862-1918), oil on canvas, 84 x 42 cm. Vienna, Upper Belvedere. © 2013. DeAgostini Picture Library/Scala, Florence

The Biblical heroine, Judith, was popular as a subject from the Middle Ages onward, where virtue overcame vice. Judith seduced General Holofernes before decapitating him in order to save her people and the city of Bethulia from the Assyrian Army. Klimt, not renowned for his portraits, used Adele Bloch-Bauer, a Viennese society woman, as the model for this work. It was this dark-haired beauty that the artist would depict in a number of his works. The other type of woman he usually portrayed was a fleshier Rubenesque-like figure. This particular depiction of the Biblical heroine (which was the predecessor of *Judith II*) rather shocked the social elite in Vienna in 1901 (although it was unveiled in Munich that same year). They were not ready for the femme fatale – a strong and wily woman clearly taking pleasure from her actions. For this reason, Viennese audiences insisted that the painting – despite its title – could not be that of Judith and was, in fact, a portrayal of Salome, the murderess. The work sold to Swiss painter, Ferdinand Hodler, soon after its completion and was framed by Klimt's brother, Georg.

The work shows an almost orgasmic Judith holding the severed head of her enemy, while she is dressed in beautiful sheer material that half hides half reveals her naked body. Her gold adornments almost "decapitate" the pious Jewish woman herself. The painting is an erotic moment in the woman's life and shows great tension and pleasure.

Love

(1895)

• Oil on canvas, 23.6 in x 17.3 in (60 cm x 44 cm)

Allegorie de l'Amour Peinture de Gustav Klimt (1862-1918), 1895. Huile sur toile. Dim: 0.60 x 0.44 m. Vienne, Wien Museum Karlsplatz. © 2013. White Images/Scala, Florence

As the title suggests, this is a beautiful depiction of love. It is a Symbolist love scene that is part of the *Allegories and Emblems* series, the purpose of which was to portray the most significant moments of life. It is an intense work divided into three sections. The couple in the love scene is central to the piece and is surrounded by a frame decorated with roses – a symbol of love – while women of differing ages overlook the loving couple. It's probably fair to assume that one of the women represents old age and impending death. It is an ethereal work that appears timeless in its approach.

Malcesine on Lake Garda

(1913)

- Oil on canvas, 43.3 in x 43.3 in (110 cm x 110 cm)

This captivating landscape of Malcesine on Lake Garda, in Italy, was destroyed by a fire in Schloss Immendorf, in Lower Austria, where it was housed for safekeeping. Unfortunately, the Nazis burned down the castle in 1945, at the end of the Second World War (1939-1945). Klimt had created the piece while staying with the Flöge family on Lake Garda on the opposite shore to Malcesine at Porto de Tremosine in 1913. Here, Klimt has captured the medieval village situated on the east coast of Lake Garda beautifully with its elevation from the water's edge to the towering castle on the hillside. The water appears to be shimmering – created with careful brushstrokes – while the buildings with their bright vibrant colors depict a tranquil life. The whole work is serene and balanced – divided into three sections comprising the lake, buildings, and castle on the hillside.

Moving Water

(1898)

Klimt, Gustav (1862-1918): Moving Water. New York, Galerie St. Etienne. Oil on canvas, 52 x 65 cm © 2013. Photo Austrian Archives/Scala, Florence

Klimt had a gift for painting water and underwater scenes. His ability to suggest movement within these subjects was simply breathtaking. Here, the underwater figures suggest a sexual association characteristic of Freud's Symbolism. Klimt had already touched on the subject in *Moving Water and Nymphs* and would return to it later in his career. All his works in this genre shimmer tirelessly, and depict the delicate movement of water and the source of all life – woman. This work could be described as erotic, and is unashamed in its portrayal of provocation.

Music

(1895)

- **Oil and golden bronze on canvas, 10.8 in x 14 in (27.5 cm x 35.5 cm)**

Klimt, Gustav (1862-1918): Die Musik. Munich, Neue Pinakothek Muenchen, Bayerische Staatsgemaeldesammlungen. Malerei / oel und Goldbronze auf Leinwand, Objektmass 27.5 x 35.5 cm (=lichtes Mass). Acc.n.: 8195. © 2013. Photo Scala, Florence/BPK, Bildagentur fuer Kunst, Kultur und Geschichte, Berlin

This captivating work is one of many of Klimt's portrayals of music – it shows the symbol of music, the lyre, and was created to represent artistic freedom. The musical woman – dressed in traditional performance attire – is meditative and engrossed in her artistic ambition. She is the dominant figure of the piece, yet is flanked by the Sphinx and the Silenus mask. (These masked figures appeared on mosaics throughout the ancient Roman world.) The work is an allegory, which it is believed helped to secure Klimt a commission with Franz Matsch for the Palais Dumba. Many commentators describe it as an early Secessionist artwork – the artists who chose to rebel against the conservative selection committee (or Kunstlerhaus) whom had the power to include, or exclude, artists of the day at their discretion.

Nuda Veritas (Naked Truth)

(1899)

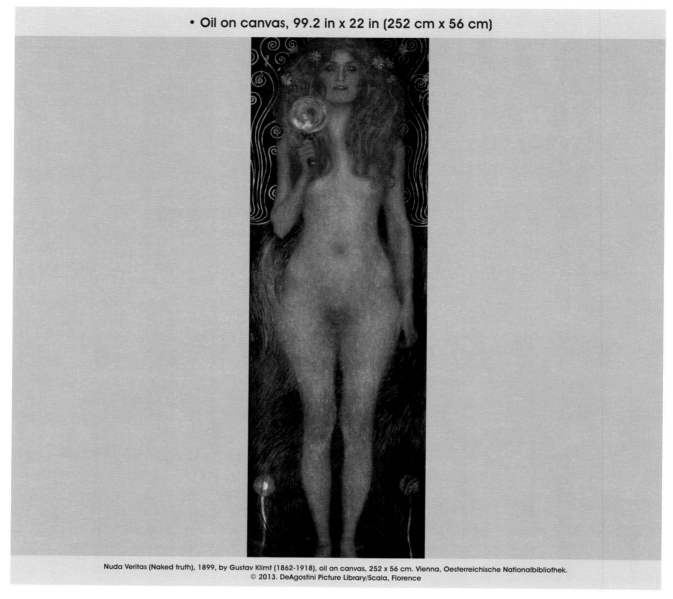

• Oil on canvas, 99.2 in x 22 in (252 cm x 56 cm)

Nuda Veritas (Naked truth), 1899, by Gustav Klimt (1862-1918), oil on canvas, 252 x 56 cm. Vienna, Oesterreichische Nationalbibliothek.
© 2013. DeAgostini Picture Library/Scala, Florence

This work, again with its beautiful naked woman, is a message by Klimt to his peers and audiences at large. It contains the quote by German poet, philosopher, historian, and playwright Friedrich Schiller: "If you can't please everyone with your deeds and your art – please only a few. To please many is bad." The words say it all really – Klimt was to incite action. The quote represents – in simplistic terms – the thinking behind the Secession movement, and as the title suggests, it was laying bare the naked truth: the truth of art. Klimt wanted people to understand that what he was trying to achieve was important. The work should not be solely concerned with the propriety of the day and the wishes and ideals of the selection committee, critics, and audiences. He wanted the freedom to express what he wanted, how he felt, who he was. Klimt, unlike other artists, was not drawn to expressing his thoughts, feelings, or life experiences in writing. He much preferred that people worked out what he had to say and who he truly was from his paintings and other works. In this painting, the young woman holds a mirror – representing the fact that the artist was inviting others (a common ideal at the time) to "Know Yourself."

Hermann Bahr, writer, dramatist, and critic, who was extensive in his writings about the Secessionist movement, left this painting, completed in 1899, to the Austrian Theater Museum.

Pallas Athena

(1898)

- **Oil on canvas, 29.5 in x 29.5 in (75 cm x 75 cm)**

Klimt, Gustav (1862-1918): Pallas Athena, 1898. Vienna, Wien Museum. Oil on canvas, 75 x 75 cm © 2013. Photo Austrian Archives/Scala, Florence

Again, a frame created by Georg Klimt, with the title clearly outlined at the top, surrounds this painting. It depicts the Goddess Athena against a backdrop of a frieze "borrowed" from an Attic vase of the 6th century BC. Athena's hair flows from the gold of the helmet to portray her feminine virtue, while the battle dress suggests her toughness. Athena was chosen as the Patron of the Viennese Secession of which the artist was the founder. She was to represent the struggle of this group of artists aiming to create an originality not seen or experienced before. Unlike Judith, in *Pallas Athena* Klimt depicts a different kind of femme fatale who is not overtly sexual but still exudes strength. It is the use of this Classical mythology that shows the artist's interest in the divine rather than the sexual. It is suggested that this is unsurprising given that Athena was portrayed as having ambiguous gender in Greek mythology. She is portrayed as an asexual Greek Goddess with extreme power. Note the *Nuda Veritas* to the bottom left of the work – the sensual emblem of truth.

The antagonistic approach to this painting, with its asexual, strong woman, did not receive the rapture it should have demanded from audiences, who were somewhat put off by its aggressive and hostile subject. It was shown at the first Secession exhibition.

Philosophy

(1899-1907)

- **Oil on canvas, 169.3 in x 118.1 in (430 x 300 cm)**

Klimt, Gustav (1862-1918): The Faculty of Philosophy – Decoration of the ceiling in the Ballroom of the University of Vienna, 1899-1907.
Presented to the public for the first time in 1900, the last version was finished in 1907. Vienna, Wien Museum. Oil on canvas, 430 x 300 cm (D105).
Lost in a fire at Immendorf castle in 1945. © 2013. Photo Austrian Archives/Scala, Florence

This magnificent painting was commissioned for the ceiling of the great hall at the University of Vienna. As already stated in the *Goldfish* entry, it never realized its ambition and was rejected by the government and university as a blatant work of pornography. Klimt began work on the painting in 1899, which showed his views at the time and his then changing style. The artist was convinced that man had lost touch with existence so the painting was planned as part of a collection that dealt with the life cycle, birth, and death, but it was seen as a pure attack on orthodox ideals. The two other paintings in the collection comprised *Medicine* and *Jurisprudence*, but the project seemed somewhat doomed from the beginning. The other painter commissioned to provide the central painting for the ceiling was Matsch. It was also his responsibility to look after the theological elements. The two artists worked in differing styles. *Philosophy* was presented in 1900 in an unfinished state at the seventh Secession exhibition held between March and June. As soon as it was unveiled – despite the fact that the university professors understood the academic reasoning behind the painting – it caused controversy and scandal. In all, 87 professors signed a petition rejecting the work. It was felt that Klimt's Symbolism in the piece was unclear. Some even felt that the painting was beyond the artist's intellect. However, Klimt was highly praised for the work by the Paris Exposition Universelle that same year. He was awarded a Gold Medal and his work ultimately approved, but due to the differences between the two commissioned artists, Klimt's work was eventually displayed in the Modern Galerie. Klimt refused his faculty commission in 1905, and with the financial support of his patron, August Lederer, he returned the monies he'd been paid. His patron received this work in return for his help. During the Second World War the collection was sent to Schloss Immendorf. It should have meant the painting was preserved, however, it was lost in the aforementioned Nazi fire.

Portrait of Adele Bloch-Bauer I

(1907)

• Oil, silver, and gold on canvas, 55.1 in x 55.1 in (140 cm x 140 cm)

Klimt, Gustav (1862-1918): Adele Bloch-Bauer I, 1907. New York, Neue Galerie New York. Oil, silver, and gold on canvas, 140 cm x 140 cm. This acquisition made available in part through the generosity of the heirs of the Estates of Ferdinand and Adele Bloch-Bauer.© 2013. Neue Galerie New York/Art Resource/Scala, Florence

This beautiful portrayal of Adele Bloch-Bauer in oil, silver, and gold, shows Klimt was influenced by Egyptian themes and art. It is the epitome of Klimt's Golden Period and consists of many geometric symbols. The work was commissioned by the model's husband, Ferdinand, and created at the height of the artist's career. It is both simplistic and ornamental in its approach. The face, hands, and neck of Adele are particularly natural and realistic, (they characterize Klimt's intimacy and are painted carefully and lovingly), while her dress, chair, and the backdrop are extremely decorative and ornate. It is widely known that Adele was one of Klimt's mistresses and, as with *Judith I*, he appears to have shown mutilation of the head and body, but separating them with decoration and neck pieces (this is evident in both works with Adele as the model and she was the only one that Klimt painted more than once). It took Klimt three years to complete the work. At the time of her death, Adele Bloch-Bauer wished the painting to be given to the Austrian State Gallery, however, the Nazis seized it during the Second World War. The painting was returned to the heirs of the Bloch-Bauer's in 2006 after a lengthy court battle. Today, this work is housed in the Neue Galerie, New York, after it was sold at auction for $135 million.

Portrait of Emilie Flöge

(1902)

• Oil on canvas, 70.1 in x 31.5 in (178 cm x 80 cm)

Klimt, Gustav (1862-1918): Portrait of Emilie Flöge, 1902. Vienna, Wien Museum. Oil on canvas, 178 x 80 cm (D126). The painting was sold to the Historisches Museum der Stadt Wien (today Wien Museum) in 1908, as it was not appreciated by Emilie nor by her mother. Klimt promised to paint a new version, but he didn't. © 2013. Photo Austrian Archives/Scala, Florence

Klimt had many lovers and fathered a large number of children, but it was with Emilie Flöge that he spent the most years of his life, though the union was never formalized. It is even unclear whether the couple had much of a sexual relationship. This exquisite oil of the artist's life-long companion is painstakingly undertaken and there is no use of Symbolism within the piece. Klimt has focused on the reality of the work and the model rather than interpretation and has painted the hands in a very real context – it was one of the ways in which he showed his love and devotion. The left hand sits snugly and comfortably on Emilie's hip, while the right hand shows her curled fingers, in a particularly natural pose, although it could be argued there is some tension in the hands. The work was completed in 1902, and is colorful with its green, blue, and purple hues. Emilie's face is lovingly painted, yet gives an appearance of being mysterious. However, Klimt's companion wasn't particularly pleased with the portrait and the work was eventually sold in 1908 to Historisches Museum der Stadt Wien (now known as the Wien Museum).

Portrait of Fritza Riedler

(1906)

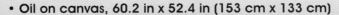

• Oil on canvas, 60.2 in x 52.4 in (153 cm x 133 cm)

Portrait of Fritza Riedler, 1906, by Gustav Klimt (1862-1918), oil on canvas, 153 x 133 cm. Vienna, Upper Belvedere. © 2013. DeAgostini Picture Library/Scala, Florence

This work, *Portrait of Fritza Riedler*, is one of Klimt's most recognized portraitures and clearly shows the geometrics that shaped many of his works. The painting has a diagonal structure, while the model, Fritza Riedler, has a flowing, tiered dress. This contrasts with the solid block colors in the background, which are square and rectangular in their approach. The work is full of decorative symbols and has an abstract quality to it, which was beginning to take shape in the artist's works. The model was the wife of the eminent engineer, Aloys Riedler, and the couple spent a great deal of time in Vienna, eventually retiring to the city. Many commentators suggest that this work is influenced by Byzantine art, with the expanse of burnt orange and gold that contrasts with the patterned chair.

Portrait of Joseph Pembauer

(1890)

• Oil on canvas, 25.6 in x 21.7 in (65 cm x 55 cm)

ANNO DOMINI· MDCCCLXXXX·

Klimt, Gustav (1862-1918): Joseph Pembauer, pianist and piano teacher, 1890. Vienna, Kunsthistorisches Museum. © 2013. Photo Austrian Archives/Scala, Florence

Unlike the previous portraiture, which could be described as abstract in its composition, this painting is a realistic portrait of pianist and teacher, Joseph Pembauer. Like the face in *Judith*, it is a very real representation of the model, who is undoubtedly framed elaborately, and contains Symbolist elements. The frame actually makes up one half of the painting. A group, known as The Pembauer Society, named for the sitter in this work, would meet in a tavern every week toward the end of the 19th century. It was here that Klimt painted the portrait, where once again, he uses the lyre to symbolize music and the arts – a fitting tribute to the model.

Portrait of Sonja Knips

(1898)

• Oil on canvas, 57.1 in x 57.1 in (145 cm x 145 cm)

Klimt, Gustav (1862-1918): Mrs. Sonja Knips, 1898. Vienna, Oesterreichische Galerie Belvedere. Oil on canvas, 145 x 145 cm. © 2013. Photo Austrian Archives/Scala, Florence

Klimt was renowned for his lifelike portraits, and this one of Sonja Knips (Baroness Poitiers des Éschelles) is no exception. The model was from the social elite and active in the Wiener Werkstatte, of which she and her husband were patrons. The portrait is another diagonal composition, complemented by the flowers (a sign of regeneration in Klimt) and contrasts between the dark brooding background and the model's light fluffy dress. By allowing herself to be painted by a controversial artist, Sonja Knips showed Klimt her support and approval for the works he was creating. But, the couple had history. Before her marriage, Sonja had been romantically linked with the artist, who had later rejected her. However, she became associated with Emilie Flöge and continued to support her former lover. What she made of this portrait, which brought Klimt great success, has to remain speculative. Having completed the work, Klimt was in huge demand for portraiture of the Vienna elite. While it is a flattering portrait of one of the aristocracy, compared to the artist's later works, which were painted in reverence to women, this painting could be considered as rather tame. There were a number of reasons for this. First, fashions changed drastically during this period, and as preferences for striking corseted dresses gave way to more liberal and looser clothing, Klimt's attitude to his portraits also changed. Mix these elements with a more liberal clientele as the years progressed and these works were to become more exciting and exposed. Klimt began to paint not what he saw, but Goddesses and femme fatales – a heady combination by early 20th-century standards.

Rose Bushes under the Trees
(c. 1905)

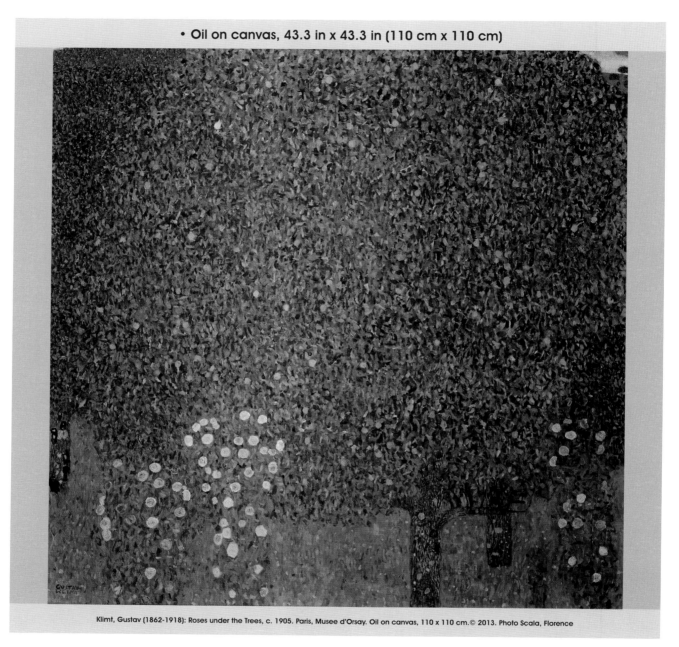

• Oil on canvas, 43.3 in x 43.3 in (110 cm x 110 cm)

Klimt, Gustav (1862-1918): Roses under the Trees, c. 1905. Paris, Musee d'Orsay. Oil on canvas, 110 x 110 cm.© 2013. Photo Scala, Florence

The trees are all consuming in this elaborate and captivating piece. The landscape could almost be considered claustrophobic in its composition. The trees really are overbearing and the rose bushes of the title seem to play a minor role. Like many of the artist's landscapes it was painted during Klimt's summer holidays at Litzlberg in 1904 and 1905. The work is carefully composed of extremely small brushstrokes, which introduce color in an intense and concentrated way (like an elaborate motif or decorative effect). As with his other works, Klimt was becoming more abstract in his approach, and the meadow and the rosebushes are secondary to the foliage that dominates the painting. The piece comprises both light and dark green hues with contrasting colors including mauves, purple, yellow, and pinks. There are tiny suggestions of the sky to the top left and right of the painting.

Schubert at the Piano

(1899)

• Oil on canvas, 59 in x 78.7 in (150 cm x 200 cm)

Klimt, Gustav (1862-1918): Schubert at the piano, 1899. Oil on canvas, 150 x 200 cm. Destroyed in Castle Immendorf fire (1945). © 2013. Photo Austrian Archives/Scala, Florence

This exquisite painting is a true lifelike reflection of the great composer, Schubert. Nikolaus Dumba, the Greek industrialist who was a great admirer of Klimt and Schubert, commissioned the piece. A patron of the arts and a music enthusiast, Dumba also commissioned Klimt to paint *Music II*. The two works were to be displayed above the doors in his music room. The work with Schubert at the piano was to become one of the artist's most well-known pieces, particularly during his own lifetime. It was also hugely popular – Schubert was a much revered composer and musician – and was probably only eclipsed by *The Kiss*. The red-haired young woman in the painting is reported to be Mizzi Zimmermann, who was pregnant with Klimt's child at the time. Klimt was also expecting to become a father again, by another woman, and was busy working up to his commission for the Faculty paintings, (also known as the University paintings), so he paid little attention to the teenager seen here. Unfortunately, the Nazis destroyed this masterpiece in 1945 when Schloss Immendorf was torched. The painting had been part of the Lederer collection sent there in 1943. Sadly, there are no precise records of how many of Klimt's paintings and great works were destroyed by retreating troops at the end of the Second World War. The main ones are known, but there were undoubtedly others housed for safety that would be burned and lost to the art world forever.

The Beethoven Frieze

(1901-1902)

- Casein paint, gold paint, black and color chalk, graphite. Applied plaster and various appliqué materials (e.g. mirror, mother-of-pearl, curtain rings, etc.), 1,344.1 in x 84.6 in (34.14 m x 2.15 m)

The Beethoven Frieze began its creation in 1901 and was displayed in the Secession building; it is still there today. Completed in 1902, it represents the final movement of Beethoven's Ninth Symphony, finished in 1824. The final movement of this fantastic and monumental symphony was choral and the first of its kind to ever grace Western music. It is considered by many to be one of the greatest choral works and symphonies ever written, widely accepted as one of the greatest works by Beethoven, and universally accepted as one of the greatest classical pieces of all time. Quite simply, it is one of the best pieces of music ever written, and for Klimt to portray it in such an exciting composition is breathtaking. This combination of two of the greatest masters of their respective days is clearly a masterpiece in creativity. It's just a shame walls don't sing.

The influences of Greek, Byzantine, early medieval, and Japanese art are clear to see in the frieze as well as the more contemporary elements, including Munch influences, that Klimt chose to include. There are strong horizontal and vertical lines within this amazing creative and ambitious project that adorn three walls. The depictions work from left to right, although note that only sections of the frieze are shown here. The first section of the wall to the left begins with symbols

Klimt, Gustav (1862-1918): The Beethoven Frieze painted for the 1902 exhibition of the Viennese Secession movement. Vienna, Secession Building. m. 13,81.
© 2013. Photo Austrian Archives/Scala, Florence

representing "a yearning for happiness," which continues in other sections of the frieze. A knight can be seen being persuaded by "mankind" to take on the fight for happiness, while the central wall encapsulates hostile forces, which are confronted. Following on from this, a sexual woman, shown in profile, stares out of the frieze provocatively. Her role is to exemplify the femme fatale so popular in art in the early 20th century. In the next painting, a red-haired figure (red hair symbolized sexual subjects for many artists at the time) is depicted to represent lasciviousness. On the final wall happiness is found through poetry, where a model is created in a long robe. Here, the artist contrasts tension and flow with differing lines.

The intention was to remove the frieze at the end of the exhibition in 1902, however, at the following exhibition, in 1903, it was decided to leave the paintings where they were. The frieze was then bought by patron, Carl Reininghaus, who sold it in 1915 to Lederer. As a Jewish citizen, Lederer lost all art works that he had collected during the Second World War, but luckily, the frieze was restored to its rightful heirs some time after the atrocities. It was then sold to the Republic of Austria in 1973. It underwent restoration that took 10 years under the direction of Manfred Koller from the Federal Office of Monuments of Vienna. In 1985, a room was given over to the frieze in the Secession building.

The Bride

(1917-1918)

• Oil on canvas (unfinished), 65.4 in x 74.8 in (166 cm x 190 cm)

Klimt, Gustav (1862-1918): The Bride, 1917-1918. Vienna, Oesterreichische Galerie Belvedere. Oil on canvas (unfinished). 166 x 190 cm. (D222).
© 2013. Photo Austrian Archives/Scala, Florence

This late painting by Klimt was unfinished at the time of his untimely death in February 1918. A semi-naked woman, whose legs are splayed out to reveal a carefully created pubic area, dominates the picture. Klimt had begun to paint symbolic ornamental shapes over the area, signaling, perhaps, his own sexual obsession. The bride from the title of the piece stands in the middle of the work with her sleeping head resting dutifully on the shoulder of the groom, while he is surrounded and almost obliterated by semi-naked women. The groom's gaze is toward the naked woman to the right of the piece rather than on his sleeping bride. There is almost an epitome here with creativity and death. Although unfinished, it is a colorful piece full of Symbolism and patterns, an allegorical piece in the modern style.

The Friends (also known as *The Women Friends* or *The Girlfriends*)

(1916-1917)

• Oil on canvas, 39 in x 39 in (99 cm x 99 cm)

The women friends, 1916-1917, by Gustav Klimt (1862-1918), oil on canvas., Private Coll. © 2013. DeAgostini Picture Library/Scala, Florence

This beautiful portrayal of two completely different looking women was another work destroyed by the Schloss Immendorf fire. Here, the artist is alluding to homosexual love, while the bodies are arguably dematerialized. Both women balance, yet dominate the piece which is set against a background of pink/red hues (unlike his earlier gold influences) and exotic birds. It is an ornamental background, enhancing the female form and shows yet another femme-fatale-styled work. The women's garments also allude to the exotic and erotic. Here is another example of how women were the artist's theme, but in this work, he suggests that women are not just the chattel and property of men, but able to love each other in their own right. Some commentators suggest that this is an ironic work; we can't see where the women's hands are. Are they clasped in each other? It's as if the truth is obvious by the very nature of what the audience is unable to see.

The Kiss

(1907-1908)

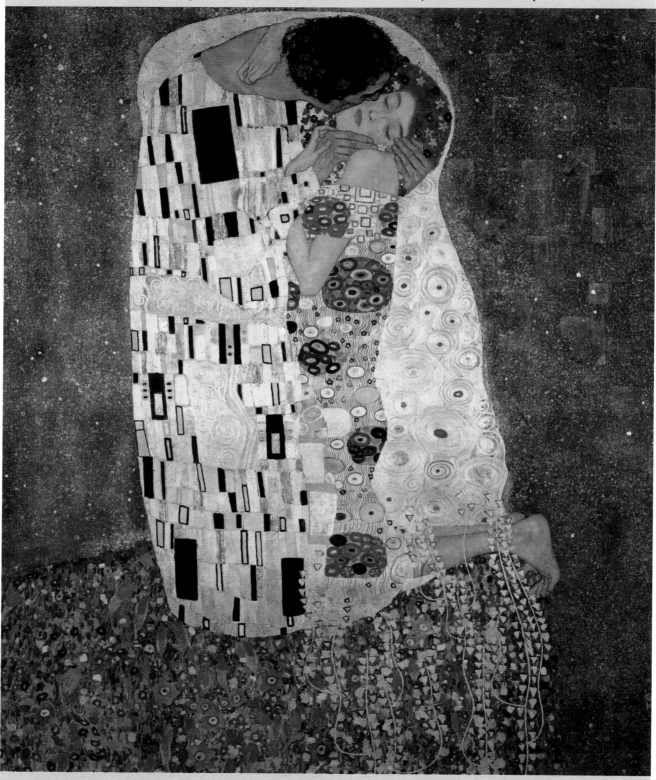

• Oil and gold leaf on canvas, 70.1 in x 70.1 in (180 cm x 180 cm)

This beautifully exquisite work, *The Kiss*, (*Der Kuss*), was started by Klimt in 1907. It is probably one of the most famous of all the artist's works. Klimt often remarked that a rest would do him "the world of good," but he also knew that taking time away from the studio was not his destiny. When creating *The Kiss* he spent just as many hours in his studio from early morning until night working, and sketch after sketch was produced in order to hone the composition. Klimt was suffering from a lack of confidence before he began work on this piece, but 1907 was to produce possibly one of the most recognized and highly acclaimed paintings in the history of art. Lovers sharing a kiss was a recurring theme for Klimt, who concentrated many of his earlier works on the theme. Here, he emphasizes the use of ornamentation and the use of gold leaf, of which he is renowned for including in many of his great masterpieces. This particular painting is a crucial part of the artist's Golden Period or Phase and is greatly influenced by his visit and travels throughout Italy in 1903 when he discovered Byzantine art and mosaics. The gold leaf undoubtedly brings this exquisite art to life. However, he was also greatly influenced by the contemporary and decorative styles that surrounded him, and being in the midst of Europe he was well aware of the Symbolism of other great artists. Though Klimt preferred not to mix or converse with his peers, he was still interested in their ideals and thought processes. He was not adverse to influences and understanding the artistic creativity that had gone before and was going on around him.

There has been much speculation over time about who the woman in the painting is. There are those who think it is Emilie, and those who identify the woman as his lover, Adele Bloch-Bauer. However, the features of the woman could be attributed to a number of women from the artist's life.

In this work, the lovers are shown embracing in a field of flowers – a common theme for the artist – where the man is bent over the woman, wrapping her in his arms while she clings on tightly. The male is depicted as strong, angular, and square. The woman is portrayed as soft and delicate, yet she remains dominant. It's her features that are important. The male's identity is almost irrelevant – other than he is needed to play the part of the lover. The couple is shrouded by a golden globe or halo as they kneel in the field covered in flowers. They are portrayed as ethereal, unearthly, and serene. It represents love, passion, and beauty.

The Austrian Gallery bought the painting in 1908, when it was first presented. It was actually unfinished at the time. Today it is the centerpiece of the largest collection of works by Klimt, and is still located in the Gallery, where Klimt's own passion for love can be enjoyed within this masterpiece. The piece was celebrated by the Austrian State in 2003 when it was depicted on a commemorative coin.

The Golden Knight (or *Life is a Struggle*)
(1903)

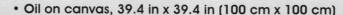

• Oil on canvas, 39.4 in x 39.4 in (100 cm x 100 cm)

Klimt, Gustav (1862-1918): Life Is a Struggle or The Golden Knight, 1903. Nagoya, Prefectural Museum of Art. Canvas, 100 x 100 cm © 2013. Photo Austrian Archives/Scala, Florence

It is suggested, by some, that the latter title for this piece, *Life is a Struggle*, is so named because Klimt was desperately reacting against the status quo within the art world. Whether this is the reason for the second title or not, it is a magnificent painting of a knight and his charger. The knight is resplendent with his lance, halter, and matching stirrups. The horse is depicted as a powerful animal – strong and unflinching. The background to the piece is intricate in composition and contrasts beautifully with the knight and horse. The knight is a conqueror; he is unworried by earthly, human elements. His is a greater calling. He sits proud and strong in the middle of the composition, supported by his equally impressive animal. Many describe this as a "glorious" composition where life and its limitations are unimportant. Even the tiny flowers in the work suggest that all is mortal (except the knight and his horse which are depicted as almost celestial). The knight appears to be looking outside the limitations of the space in which he rests, waiting for something more important than the life that surrounds him and shows him admiration. He is unfazed by the adoration and is seeking something out of sight, yet within his grasp.

The Old Burgtheater

(1887-1888)

• Watercolor, gouache, gold, 35.9 in x 40.6 in (91.2 cm x 103 cm)

Klimt, Gustav (1862-1918): Auditorium in the 'Altes Burgtheater', the old Court Theatre, replaced by a new building in 1888. Vienna, Kunsthistorisches Museum. Oil on canvas.
© 2013. Photo Austrian Archives/Scala, Florence

This work, *The Old Burgtheater*, is so realistically composed that it's hard not to imagine being in the theater while surveying the painting. It was commissioned in 1887, by the Municipal Court of Vienna, when the theater's last performance took place in October the following year. Klimt painted several versions of the work, but this particular portrayal won The Golden Order of Merit (The Emperor's Prize award by Franz Joseph), also known as the Golden Cross for Artist Merit. The work is so carefully created that the perspective is incredibly real, and it is cited that Klimt had to create his work on the precise measurements of the theater that he'd had to take himself. He was presented with a season ticket for the theater's performances and was a willing audience member. Rather than watching the performance, Klimt has captured the theater auditorium and around 240 spectators (many of whom were recognizable patrons of the day) with such realism that we, as the audience, are invited to watch the audience as they settle for a performance. The upper echelons of Vienna's elite were desperate to be in the painting. Everybody that was anybody wanted to be painted within the auditorium. The mayor, it was noted, was missing from the original work and had to be painted in afterward. The honor that Klimt attained for this masterpiece would ensure his place in the world of art, despite the fact that later works would bring him much controversy.

The Park

(1910 or earlier)

- **Oil on canvas, 43.5 in x 43.5 in (110.4 cm x 110.4 cm)**

This intense, but exquisite, piece was a move toward abstraction by Klimt, which represents the life cycle of nature. The foliage is overwhelming, yet carefully crafted, and brings a real beauty and delicacy to the work, infused with a multitude of colors. The landscape is a close-up of the subject matter – quite typical of the artist's portrayals of this genre – and is reminiscent of the mosaics, which encapsulate and dominate his work in equal measure. This work is beautifully balanced by both naturalism and ornamental elements that combine to bring *The Park* to life.

The Sunflower

(1907)

- Oil on canvas, 43.3 in x 43.3 in (110 cm x 110 cm)

Klimt, Gustav (1862-1918): Sunflower, 1906-1907. Oil on canvas – D146. © 2013. Photo Austrian Archives/Scala, Florence

Klimt's *The Sunflower* might bring Van Gogh's still life paintings to mind, but this is so different. Rather than being arranged in a vase, it is painted in the field, or garden, where it grows. There is no decay here – the plant is composed in all its glory. It is a stunning landscape of meadow flowers with a tall protruding sunflower rising steadily toward a sun that can only be imagined. Its head is bowed to the surroundings in which it grows. Like *The Kiss,* this 1907 work was first presented at the Art Show Vienna in 1908. That's not all the works have in common – notice how the sunflower looks as though its form resembles that of the lovers in *The Kiss.* This painting clearly shows the artist's love for nature – the pureness of the piece is geometric and opulent, yet humbling too.

The Three Ages of Woman
(1905)

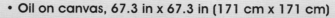
• Oil on canvas, 67.3 in x 67.3 in (171 cm x 171 cm)

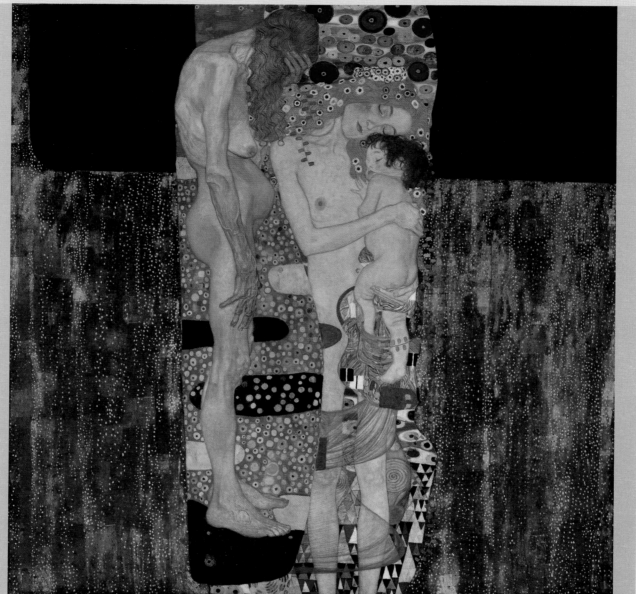

Klimt, Gustav (1862-1918): The Three Ages of Woman, 1905. Rome, National Gallery of Modern Art (GNAM). Painting 171 x 171 cm. Inv.: 951.
© 2013. Photo Scala, Florence – courtesy of the Ministero Beni e Att. Culturali

In 1911, *The Three Ages of Woman* won the Gold Medal at the International Exhibition. It is an allegorical work dedicated to the life stages of a woman: infancy, motherhood, and old age. A young girl is shown shrouded by protection in the arms of a young woman. Next to them, to the left of the piece, an older woman stands facing them, head bowed, while covering her eyes with one hand. This particular figure is based on Rodin's statue, *The Old Courtesan*, which was part of the Secession exhibition of 1901. Klimt was greatly influenced by this and other works by Rodin. The two men met in 1902 when Rodin was visiting Vienna – he was impressed with *The Beethoven Frieze*. The background to the work is unusual for Klimt at this time, (although this later became synonymous with the artist) with its dark hues, but it was his first oil painting in large scale, and his first allegory that did not include mythical or historical figures.

This painting was bought by Galleria Nazionale d'Arte Moderna in Rome in 1912.

The Virgin

(1913)

- Oil on canvas, 74.8 in x 78.7 in (190 cm x 200 cm)

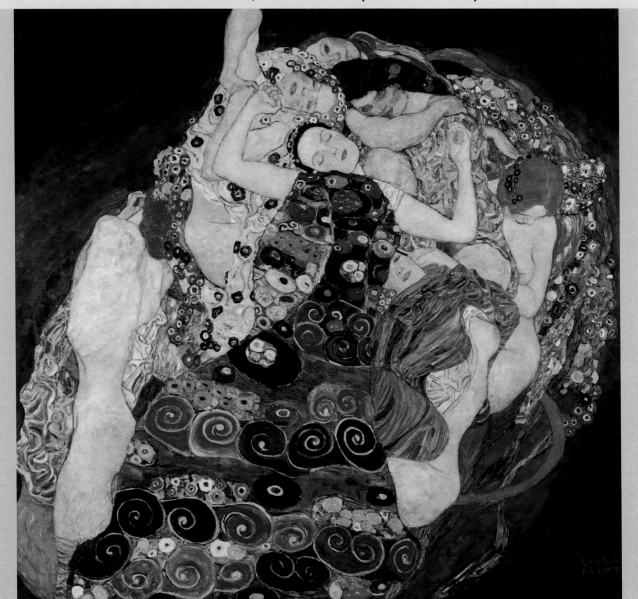

Klimt, Gustav (1862-1918): The Virgin, 1913. Prague, National Gallery (Narodni Galeri). Oil on canvas, 190 x 200 cm (D184). © 2013. Photo Austrian Archives/Scala, Florence

This work is composed of many flowers – a common motif in Klimt's work – and suggests regeneration, or the journey to womanhood. The women in the painting appear intertwined. The different stages of life are presented, and dislocated body parts appear as if they are almost under water, or floating in some way. This painting focuses on awakening.

Theater in Taormina (detail from wall decoration)

(1886-1888)

- Oil/stucco, 295.3 in x 157.5 in (750 cm x 400 cm)

Klimt, Gustav (1862-1918): Theater in Taormina (detail from wall decoration), 1886-88. Vienna, Burgtheater. Oil/Stucco, D41. © 2013. Photo Austrian Archives/Scala, Florence

This exciting work has a photographic precision and quality to it, which is stunning. Klimt was moving away from the styles of other painters to create his own distinctive works. Klimt was commissioned – alongside his brother Ernst and Franz Matsch – as part of painting the historical scenes for the new Burgtheater (due for completion in 1886). The artists were preparing works for the tympanum and the stairway ceilings. However, Klimt was influenced by Hans Makart and became interested in realism. *Theater in Taormina* shows incredible detail in the pillars (note the right of the piece – they almost appear to shimmer) and the flooring – including the carpets – and the hazy background. In the carpets, Klimt captures the weave perfectly, however, the theater was in ruins when Klimt had to work this piece from his imagination.

Water Serpents I

(1904-1907)

• **Mixed media and gold on vellum, 19.7 in x 7.9 in (50 cm x 20 cm)**

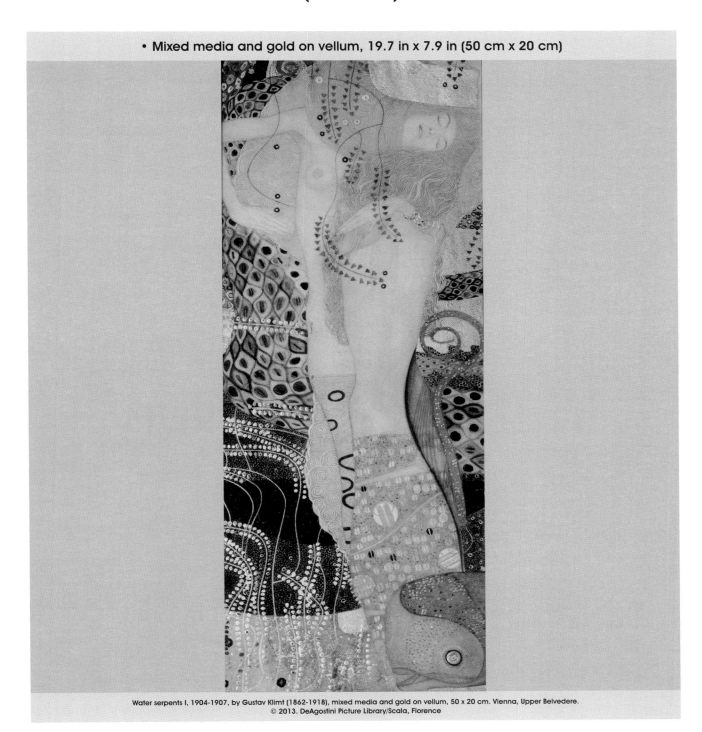

Water serpents I, 1904-1907, by Gustav Klimt (1862-1918), mixed media and gold on vellum, 50 x 20 cm. Vienna, Upper Belvedere.
© 2013. DeAgostini Picture Library/Scala, Florence

Water Serpents I and *Water Serpents II* see Klimt return to a theme of sensual woman depicted in water. This particular piece is unusual in its coloring, which is dictated by the mixed media and gold on parchment. It differs only from the early sketches for the work in that the gold paint has been added. The "thread" entwining the women's bodies, the fact that they are under water, shown with a water serpent, and the piece is allegorical meant that Klimt would not be accused of an unsuitable theme when this work was presented to an Austrian audience. It is an engaging work, showing his highly innovative creativity at this time. The second depiction of this theme is better known, however, both works helped to define Klimt – and his theme of sensual women – with their elaborate detail and realism.

Klimt

In The 21ˢᵗ Century

(PA Photos)

■ **ABOVE: Visitors admire paintings by art nouveau master Gustav Klimt:** *Adele Bloch-Bauer*, **left, and** *Hauser in Unterach am Attersee*, **right, in Vienna's Belvedere Gallery.**

To experience the works of Klimt, and for an insight in to this exceptional artist, the best place to start is in Vienna itself. The Burgtheater houses four ceiling paintings and there are sketches in the Klimt Room. It is possible to view these either by a visit to the theater or when taking in a performance. The Austrian Theater Museum is also well worth a visit. Here, you will find the *Nuda Veritas*, while Belvedere Castle owns the world's largest collection of Klimt paintings. Housed in Belvedere are *The Kiss, The Sunflower*, and *Family* – a fairly recent addition in 2012.

The Kunsthistorisches Museum in Vienna is an artistically staged building, which boasts Klimt's work as part of its interior. In 2012, the museum held an exhibition of Klimt's works that continued into January 2013. The exhibition displayed 13 masterpieces by Klimt, completed for the grand staircase as its focus. The Wien Museum houses around 400 drawings and has the world's largest collection of Klimt sketches (including preparatory pieces), covering all periods in the artist's career. Another reason to visit Austria is the Vienna Secession, built by Joseph Maria Olbrich, with its golden laurel leaf dome. Today, the Secession is one of the most visited buildings in Austria and houses *The Beethoven Frieze,* which is carefully preserved in a specially built room. Other museums include the Albertina and the Leopold.

Between 1911 and his death in 1918, Klimt worked in his studio, which was reopened to the public in 2012 following renovation work. The house itself can be found in Vienna's 13th district on Feldmühlgasse. This particular memorial dedicated to the artist will give the appreciative viewer a feel for the life and times of Gustav Klimt. While today Klimt is highly celebrated and remains a popular artist on a global scale, his work was neglected throughout much of the 20th century. He never married – although he fathered a large number of children – and he was averse to using himself as subject matter. There are no self-portraits of this great artist. He was a relatively private man – he was not intent on writing his thought processes with regard to his work – and was discreet about his relationships and family. Apart from upsetting the establishment with his unfairly termed "pornographic" works, he did not claim, or set out to revolutionize, the art world in any way. However, the founding of the highly influential Vienna Secession was simply groundbreaking and Klimt leaves behind a legacy of the largest number of works dedicated to the sensuality of women. He helped to establish Vienna as one of the leading centers for culture and the arts – although his own influence on a younger generation of artists and any subsequent movements was fairly limited. He produced a striking number of works combining the new and the old, the cycle of life, regeneration, realism, the beauty of nature, and the abstract. Some commentators suggest that while Klimt is an extremely important and popular artist, in terms of art history, he remains unimportant. While that may be so, in the middle of the first decade of the 21st century the Jewish descendants of one former owner were claiming back their "inheritance," five paintings by Klimt, estimated at the time to be worth around $150 million. Many of Klimt's works were claimed by the Austrian state – from their rightful owners – during the annexation of the country and the rise of the Nazis, who stole hundreds of thousands of pieces of art in the decade prior to the start of the Second World War. A large number of his works were needlessly (and deliberately) destroyed by retreating Nazis at the end of the war, however, where possible, his paintings have been reinstated with the heirs of their former owners. While he may not have inspired generations of artists, Klimt has influenced the likes of designer John Galliano, who based the Christian Dior 2008 collection on his works.

Symbolism began its existence in literature before it diverged in to other art mediums. Klimt became one of the greatest exponents of Symbolism and, today, poets, authors, and writers cite Klimt as a huge influence on their works. *Goldfish* was the influence for the 2012 album cover of Japanese rock band, Buck-Tick's new release, *Yume Miru Uchuu*. Klimt's 150th birthday celebrations in 2012 were widespread: in the United States, the Neue Galerie in New York celebrated with a special exhibition.

(PA Photos)

■ **ABOVE:** The Kunsthistorisches (Fine Arts) Museum on the far side of the Maria-Theresien-Platz.

■ **LEFT:** Inside an atelier used by Klimt. It was opened to the public in Vienna in 2012.

(PA Photos)

The museum is located at the southeast corner of Fifth Avenue and East 86th Street. Works including *Pale Face* (1903), *Adele Bloch-Bauer* (1907), *The Black Feather Hat* (1910), *The Park of Schloss Kammer* (1910), *Forester House in Weissenbach on the Attersee* (1914), *Forest Slope in Unterach on the Attersee* (1916), and *The Dancer* (1916-1918) were all on display, alongside some rare and unseen photographs of Klimt with Emilie Flöge, in the summer of 2012. A number of drawings were also included which comprised a group of studies from the three paintings for the University of Vienna (or Faculty paintings), and sketches for the Vienna Secession of 1902. As well as the exhibition, the Neue Galerie celebrated Klimt throughout the building – including a specially made Klimt cake in one of its cafés, and gold and silver cufflinks offered for sale by The Design Shop, based on the design by Josef Hoffmann (and made for Klimt). The Book Store also took part in the Klimt celebrations with *The Lady in Gold* by Anne-Marie O'Connor and *The Age of Insight* by Eric Kandel. Elsewhere, commemorative coins were issued, guided walking tours were organized (in Vienna), and Google celebrated with a Gustav Klimt doodle of *The Kiss*.

Klimt lived much of his life as a recluse, yet today, his works sell for millions of dollars. What the artist himself would have made of his status in today's world can only be given over to speculation, but as a prolific painter of allegorical works, perhaps there's something in that?

(PA Photos)

■ **ABOVE:** An atelier used by Austrian painter Gustav Klimt is open for public viewing in Vienna in 2012.

■ **OPPOSITE:** A model presents a creation by British designer John Galliano for Christian Dior's Haute-Couture Spring-Summer 2008 collection. Galliano was influenced by Klimt.

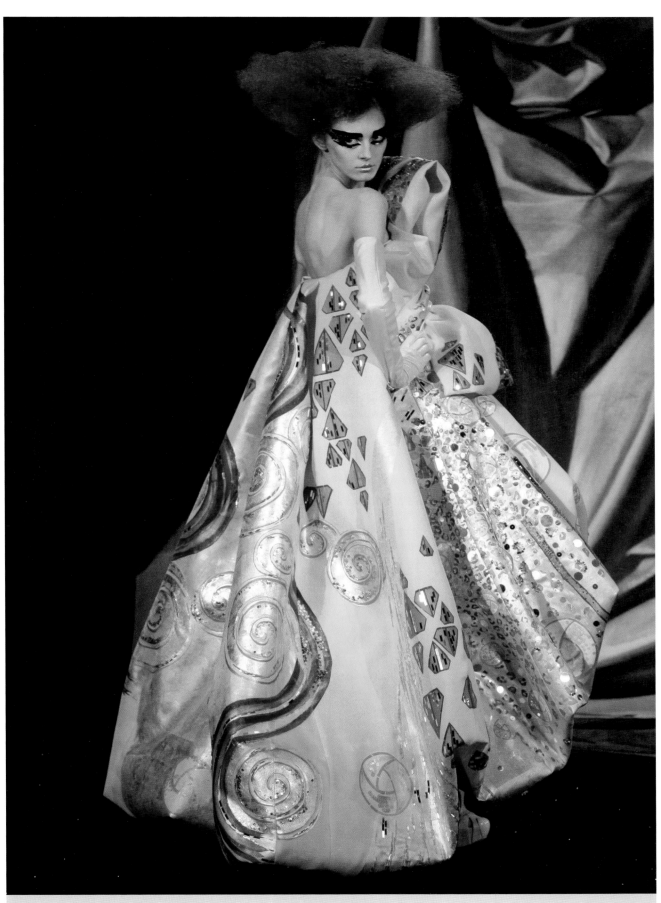

(PA Photos)

(PA Photos)

■ **ABOVE:** Neue Galerie, a museum of German and Austrian art, in New York.

Books

Gustav Klimt: 1862-1918, Rachel Barnes (October 2010)

Gustav Klimt – The Complete Paintings, Tobias G. Natter (September 2012)

Gustav Klimt 1862-1918 (Basic Art Album), Gilles Neret (May 2000)

Gustav KLIMT, 2013, Gustav Klimt (July 2012)

Gustav Klimt: Landscapes, Stephan Koja (2007)

Gustav Klimt: Art Nouveau Visionary, Eva di Stefano (November 2008)

Gustav Klimt 2013 (Fine Art), Gustav Klimt (August 2012)

Gustav Klimt: Drawings & Watercolours: Drawings and Watercolours, Rainer Metzger (November 2005)

Klimt, Alfred Weidinger (October 2007)